SOME DISTINCTIVE
FEATURES OF ISLAM

OTHER BOOKS BY THE SAME AUTHOR

Absolute Justice, Kindness and Kinship—
The Three Creative Principles

Christianity—A Journey from Facts to Fiction

An Elementary Study of Islam

The Gulf Crisis and the New World Order

Homeopathy: Like Cures Like

Islam's Response to Contemporary Issues

Murder in the Name of Allah

Revelation, Rationality, Knowledge and Truth

The Seal of the Prophets, His Personality and Character

The True Islamic Concept of Jihad

The Truth about the Alleged Punishment
for Apostasy in Islam

With Love to the Muslims of the World

ABOUT THE AUTHOR

Ḥaḍrat Mirza Tahir Ahmad (1928–2003), may Allah have infinite mercy on his soul, a man of God, Voice articulate of the age, a great orator, a deeply learned scholar of phenomenal intelligence, a prolific and versatile writer, a keen student of comparative religions was loved and devoutly followed by his more than 10 million Ahmadi Muslim followers all over the world as their Imam, the spiritual head, being the fourth successor of Ḥaḍrat Mirza Ghulam Ahmad (the Promised Messiah and Mahdi[as]), to which august office he was elected as Khalīfatul Masīḥ in 1982.

After the promulgation of general Zia-ul-Haq anti-Ahmadiyya Ordinance of 26th April 1984 he had to leave his beloved country, Pakistan, and migrated to England from where he launched Muslim Television Ahmadiyya International (MTA) which would (and still does) telecast its programmes 24 hours a day to the four corners of the world.

Besides being a religious leader, he was a homeopathic physician of world fame, a highly gifted poet and a sportsman.

He had his schooling in Qadian, India, and later joined the Govt. College, Lahore, Pakistan, and after graduating from Jāmi‘ah Ahmadiyya, Rabwah, Pakistan with distinction, he obtained his honours degree in Arabic from the Punjab University, Lahore. From 1955 to 1957 he studied at the School of Oriental and African Studies, University of London.

He had a divinely inspired and very deep knowledge of the Holy Quran which he translated into Urdu. He also partially revised and added explanatory notes to the English translation of the Holy Quran by Ḥaḍrat Maulawī Sher Ali[ra]. *Revelation, Rationality, Knowledge and Truth* is his magnum opus.

Though he had no formal education in philosophy and science, he had a philosophical bent of mind and tackled most difficult and abstruse theological-philosophical questions with great acumen and ease and his intellectual approach was always rational and scientific. For a layman he had an amazingly in-depth knowledge of science, especially life sciences which attracted him most. He also had deep knowledge of human psychology. His was an analytical mind of high intelligence—an intellect scintillating with brilliance, capable of solving knottiest problems with ease, leaving his listeners and readers spellbound.

SOME DISTINCTIVE FEATURES OF ISLAM

Mirza Tahir Ahmad

ISLAM INTERNATIONAL PUBLICATIONS LTD.

TILFORD, SURREY

Some Distinctive Features of Islam
by Mirza Tahir Ahmad

Copyright by Islam International Publications Ltd.

First published in English 1985
Reprinted 1987, 1989, 1992, 1995, 2007, 2012 (ISBN: 1 85372 052 6)
Reprinted in 2017

Published by
Islam International Publications Ltd.
Islamabad, Sheephatch Lane
Tilford, Surrey GU10 2AQ

Printed in UK at
Raqeem Press
Farnham, Surrey

Cover design by Salman Muhammad Sajid
Book layout and index prepared by Dr. Abdul Majid Shah

ISBN: 978-1-84880-895-9
13 12 11 10 9 8

CONTENTS

PUBLISHER'S NOTE

According to our system of counting Quranic verses, the verse *Bismillāh irraḥmān irraḥīm* (In the name of Allah, the Most Gracious, Ever Merciful) is counted as the first verse of the chapter, which it precedes. Some publishers of the Holy Quran however, begin counting following *Bismillāh irraḥmān irraḥīm*. Should the reader not find the relevant verse under the number mentioned in this book, he or she is advised to deduct 1 from the number. For example, if this book quotes Ch. 35: *Al-Fāṭir:* 25, then some copies of the Holy Quran will list the same verse under Ch. 35: *Al-Fāṭir:* 24.

Where necessary, translation of the Arabic text has been elaborated by additional words to explain the meaning. Such words are not in italics. The word *and* at the commencement of a translated verse has been omitted.

The form *ibn* has been used in both initial and medial position in the names of persons, in order to conform to current usage, although *bin* also occurs medially in some original texts (abbreviated usually as *b.*).

Quotations from the Holy Bible are from the New World Translation.

The name of Muhammad^{sa}, the Holy Prophet of Islam, has been followed by the symbol ^{sa}, which is an abbreviation for the prayer (ﷺ) *Ṣallallāhu 'Alaihi Wasallam* (may peace and blessings of Allah be upon him). The names of other Prophets^{as} and messengers are followed by the symbol ^{as}, an abbreviation for (عليه السلام/عليهم السلام) *'Alaihissalām/ Alaihimussalām* (on whom be peace). The actual prayers have not generally been set out in full, but they should nevertheless, be understood as being repeated in full in each case. The symbol ^{ra} is used with the name of the Companions of the Holy Prophet^{sa} and those of the Promised Messiah^{as}. It stands for (رضي الله عنه/عنها/عنهم) *Raḍī Allāhu 'anhu/'anhā/'anhum* (may Allah be pleased with him/with her/with them). ^{rh} stands for (رحمه الله تعالى) *Raḥimahullāhu Ta'ālā* (may Allah's blessing be on him). ^{at} stands for (ايده الله تعالى) *Ayyadahullāhu Ta'ālā* (may Allah, the Almighty help him).

In transliterating Arabic words we have followed the following system adopted by the Royal Asiatic Society:

ا	at the beginning of a word, pronounced as *a, i, u* preceded by a very slight aspiration, like *h* in the English word *honour*.
ث	*th*, pronounced like *th* in the English word *thing*.
ح	*ḥ*, a guttural aspirate, stronger than *h*.
خ	*kh*, pronounced like the Scotch *ch* in *loch*.
ذ	*dh*, pronounced like the English *th* in *that*.
ص	*ṣ*, strongly articulated *s*.
ض	*ḍ*, similar to the English *th* in *this*.
ط	*ṭ*, strongly articulated palatal *t*.
ظ	*ẓ*, strongly articulated *z*.
ع	*'*, a strong guttural, the pronunciation of which must be learnt by the ear.

غ   *gh*, a sound approached very nearly in the *r grasseye* in French, and in the German *r*. It requires the muscles of the throat to be in the 'gargling' position whilst pronouncing it.

ق   *q*, a deep guttural *k* sound.

ئ   ', a sort of catch in the voice.

Short vowels are represented by:

a for ———— (like *u* in *bud*)

i for ———— (like *i* in *bid*)

u for ———— (like *oo* in *wood*)

Long vowels by:

ā for ———— or آ (like *a* in *father*);

ī for ى ———— or ———— (like *ee* in *deep*);

ū for و ———— (like *oo* in *root*);

Other:

ai for ى ———— (like *i* in *site*)*;

au for و ———— (resembling *ou* in *sound*)

Please note that in transliterated words the letter *e* is to be pronounced as in *prey* which rhymes with *day*; however the pronunciation is flat without the element of English diphthong. If in Urdu and Persian words *e* is lengthened a bit more, it is transliterated as *ei* to be pronounced as *ei* in *feign* without the element of diphthong.

---

* In Arabic words like شیخ (Shaikh) there is an element of diphthong which is missing when the word is pronounced in Urdu.

Thus ک is transliterated as *kei*. For the nasal sound of *n* we have used the symbol *ń*. Thus the Urdu word میں is transliterated as *meiń*.*

The consonants not included in the above list have the same phonetic value as in the principal languages of Europe.

We have not transliterated Arabic words which have become part of English language, e.g., Islam, Mahdi, Quran†, Hijra, Ramadan, Hadith, ulama, umma, sunna, kafir, pukka, etc..

Curved commas are used in the system of transliteration, ' for ع, ' for ء. Commas as punctuation marks are used according to the normal usage. Similarly, normal usage is followed for the apostrophe.

---

* These transliterations are not included in the system of transliteration by The Royal Asiatic Society.

† Concise Oxford Dictionary records Quran in three forms—Quran, Qur'an and Koran.

FOREWORD TO THE PRESENT EDITION

Some Distinctive Features of Islam was a lecture delivered by Ḥaḍrat Mirza Tahir Ahmad[rh], Khalifatul Masih IV, of blessed memory at the University of Canberra, Australia. It was first published in UK in 1985 and then in 1987, 1989, 1992, and 1995 respectively four more editions of it were published in UK. Now it is being published again.

The speaker builds up his lecture on the thesis that the most distinctive feature of Islam is twofold: first, it is the only religion which claims to be, and is, the final, the universal and eternal religion for all times and for all peoples, second, it is the only religion which acknowledges, and bears witness to, the veracity of every other religions and claims that the truth is not the monopoly of Islam alone—whereas every other religion claims that it alone contains the Divine truth. Then Hadrat Mirza Tahir Ahmad[rh] answers at some length the question that if all religions are from God then why is there any difference in religions. Moreover he argues that Islamic teachings are not only universal and eternal but are also complete, comprehensive and perfect, and that the Holy Quran is the final and immutable word of God free from all human interpolation; and that the Prophet of Islam, the Holy Prophet Muhammad[sa] is the Seal of the

Prophets and the best of them and the perfect model of excellence for mankind.

In the middle part of lecture he discuses seventeen features of Islam which distinguish it from other religions and ideologies including the Islamic concept of justice and Islamic teachings regarding the form and function of government.

At the end the speaker introduces the Founder of Ahmadiyya Jama'at and the Jama'at itself to his audience concluding his lecture with an excerpt from the writings of the Promised Messiah[as].

Mirza Anas Ahmad
M.A. M. Litt. (OXON)
Wakilul Isha'at
Rabwah
May 31, 2006

SOME DISTINCTIVE
FEATURES OF ISLAM

اَشْهَدُ اَنْ لَّا اِلٰهَ اِلَّا اللّٰهُ وَحْدَهُ لَا شَرِيكَ لَهُ وَ

اَشْهَدُ اَنَّ مُحَـمَّـدًا عَبْدُهُ وَ رَسُوْلُـهُ

اَمَّا بَعْدُ فَاَعُوْذُ بِاللّٰهِ مِنَ الشَّيْطٰنِ الرَّجِيْمِ

بِسْمِ اللّٰهِ الرَّحْمٰنِ الرَّحِيْمِ ۞
اَلْحَمْدُ لِلّٰهِ رَبِّ الْعٰلَمِيْنَ ۞ الرَّحْمٰنِ الرَّحِيْمِ ۞
مٰلِكِ يَوْمِ الدِّيْنِ ۞
اِيَّاكَ نَعْبُدُ وَ اِيَّاكَ نَسْتَعِيْنُ ۞
اِهْدِنَا الصِّرَاطَ الْمُسْتَقِيْمَ ۞
صِرَاطَ الَّذِيْنَ اَنْعَمْتَ عَلَيْهِمْ ۙ
غَيْرِ الْمَغْضُوْبِ عَلَيْهِمْ وَلَا الضَّآلِّيْنَ ۞   *

AFTER THE TRADITIONAL RECITATION and reciting the *Surah Al-Fātiḥa* (the opening chapter of the Holy Quran), the Head of Jamāʿat Ahmadiyya commenced as follows:

---

* I bear witness that there is no god but Allah, the One, and I bear witness that Muhammad is His servant and messenger. After that I seek refuge with Allah from Satan, the rejected. In the name of Allah, the Gracious, the Merciful. All praise belongs to Allah, Lord of all the worlds, the Gracious, the Merciful, Master of the Day of Judgement. Thee alone do we worship and Thee alone do we implore for help. Guide us in the right path—the path of those on whom Thou hast bestowed Thy blessings, those who have not incurred Thy displeasure, and those who have not gone astray. [Publisher]

No Monopoly of Truth

While speaking on the subject of the distinctive features of Islam, the first and most attractive feature that strikes one, is its most endearing disclaimer that Islam denies having a monopoly of truth, and that there have been no other true religions. Nor does it claim that Arabs alone have been the recipients of God's love. Islam is the only religion that totally rejects the notion that truth is the monopoly of any single faith, race or people; instead it professes that Divine guidance is a general bounty that has sustained humanity in all ages. The Holy Quran tells us that there is neither a race nor a people, who have not been blessed with the bounty of Divine guidance, and there is neither a region of the earth nor a body of people who have not received Prophets and Messengers of God.[1]

Contrary to this worldwide Islamic view of the manifestation of Allah's favour upon all people of the earth we are struck by the fact that no Book of any other religion verifies or even mentions the possibility of other peoples and nations having received light and guidance from Allah at any stage in history. In fact, the truth and validity of a local or regional religion is often emphasised so greatly, and the truth of other faiths ignored so totally, as if the sun of truth had only risen and set upon the limited horizon of certain people to the exclusion of the rest of the world, so to say, abandoned and condemned to eternal darkness. For instance, the Bible presents only the God of Israel, and it repeatedly says:

Blessed be the Lord, the God of Israel.[2]

It does not, even in passing, verify the truth of religious revelations bestowed on other lands and upon other peoples. Thus, the belief of the Jews that all Israelite Prophets were sent only to the tribes of Israel is in full conformity with the intent and message of the Bible. Jesus[as] had also declared that his advent was intended for the guidance of the Hebrew tribes alone, and had said, I was sent only to the lost sheep of the house of Israel,[3] and he admonished his disciples in the words: 'Do not give dogs what is holy, and do not throw your pearls before swine.'[4]

Similarly, the Hindu religion also addresses its books only to those of high birth. It is said, 'If one of base birth should per chance hear a text of the Vedas, the King should seal his ears with molten wax and lead. And should he recite a portion of the scripture, his tongue should be severed; and should he succeed in reading the Veda, his body should be hacked to pieces.'[5]

Even if we disregard such drastic injunctions, or offer some less severe explanation of them, the fact remains that the holy books of various faiths do not, even by implication, allude to the truth of the religions of other lands and peoples. The basic question that arises here is that if all these faiths were in fact true, then what was the wisdom in presenting the concept of God in such limited and restricted terms? The Holy Quran readily furnishes a solution of this predicament. It says that even before the revelation of the Holy Quran and the advent of the Holy Prophet Muhammad[sa], divine Messengers had indeed been sent to every nation and every part of the globe, but their sphere was regional and their assignments temporary. This is because human civilisation had not yet reached a stage of development which merited the commissioning of a universal messenger, bearing a universal message.

A Universal Religion

The very first leaf of the Holy Quran praises the Lord Who is the Sustainer of all the worlds, and its last passage urges us to pray to the Lord of mankind. Thus, both the first and the last words of the Holy Quran present the concept of the entire universe, and not merely that of a God of the Arabs or the Muslims. Verily, no one before the Holy Prophet[sa] of Islam had beckoned the whole of humanity, and no book before the Holy Quran had addressed the entire world. The first such claim was made in favour of the Holy Prophet[sa] of Islam in these words:

> And We have not sent thee but as a bearer of glad tidings and a Warner, for all mankind, but most men know not.[6]

And then:

> Say, 'O mankind! Truly I am a Messenger to you all.'[7]

And when the Holy Quran calls itself *a message for all the worlds*[8], it upholds itself as the guidance with which is linked the true development and advancement of mankind.

The Holy Quran has repeatedly been called the Verifier of other Books and Muslims are admonished to believe in all other Prophets[as] in exactly the same manner as they believe in their own Prophet[sa]. In our faith, it is forbidden to make a distinction among any of them, much less to believe in some and reject others. The Holy Quran says:

All (of us) believe in Allah, and in His angels, and in His Books, and in His Messengers.[9]

It may not be without merit to examine if universality in itself is a desirable feature, and why Islam has laid such great stress upon it. Ever since Islam has brought the message of the unity of mankind, the pace of the march towards such unity has continued to accelerate in every sphere. An example of this march in our times is the establishment of different international bodies and federations. Indeed, these are but milestones along the long and devious journey towards unity among all mankind. So, the need that is keenly felt by the advanced and civilised man of today had already been fulfilled by planting the seed of its solution in the message of Islam 1400 years ago. Today, of course, the rapid development of travel and communication has lent a new impetus to the march towards unity among peoples and nations.

Differences and Contradictions among Faiths – Their Reality

A question that arises is: if all religions were in fact founded by Messengers[as] from God, then why is there any difference in their teachings? Can the same God sends own different teachings?

This question is answered by Islam alone, and this, too, is a distinctive feature of this religion. Islam holds that there are two basic causes of differences between various religions. First, that varying conditions had needed varying dictates and rules, and the All-Knowing and All-Wise God had provided guidance for different ages, regions and peoples in accordance with their respective needs. Second, the contents of various faiths faded and wilted under the vicissitudes of time; hence they were not preserved in their original form. In some cases, the followers themselves introduced innovations and variations to suit changing needs, and the originally revealed Books continued to be interpolated for this purpose. Obviously, such adulteration of the Divine Message ultimately mandated fresh guidance from the Original Source. As God has said in the Holy Quran:

> *They pervert the words from their proper places and have forgotten a good part of that with which they were exhorted.*[10]

If we examine the history of differences between various faiths in the light of the principles enunciated by the Holy Quran, we find that the differences tend to diminish as we reach nearer the source itself. For instance, if we limit the comparison of Christianity and Islam only to the life of Jesus[as] and the four gospels in the Bible, then there will appear only very minor differences between the basic teachings of the Bible and the Holy Quran. But, as we travel further down the road of time, the chasm of these differences becomes wider and wider, till it becomes totally unbridgeable—and all because of human endeavour to revise that which was originally revealed. The history of other faiths also reveals the same basic reality, and we find strong corroboration of the Quranic view, that the direction of human changes and revisions of the Divine Message, has always been from the worship of one God to that of several, and from reality to fiction, from humanity to deification of human beings.

The Holy Quran tells us that the surest way to distinguish a true religion, despite its subsequent mutilation, is to examine its origin. If the origin reveals the teaching of the unity of God, worship of none save the One God, and a true and genuine sympathy for all humanity, then such a religion, despite subsequent changes, must be accepted as true. The founders of religions that satisfy this criterion were indeed righteous and pious beings, and true Messengers deputed by God, between whom we should make no distinction and in whose truth we must believe fully. They have certain fundamental features common to all regardless of differences in time and place. Thus expounds the Holy Quran:

وَمَآ أُمِرُوٓا إِلَّا لِيَعۡبُدُوا اللَّهَ مُخۡلِصِينَ لَهُ الدِّينَ ۚ حُنَفَآءَ وَ
يُقِيمُوا الصَّلَوٰةَ وَيُؤۡتُوا الزَّكَوٰةَ وَذَٰلِكَ دِينُ الۡقَيِّمَةِ ۚ

And they were not commanded but to serve Allah, being sincere to Him in obedience, and being upright, and to observe Prayer, and pay the Zakat. And that is the religion of the people of the right path.[11]

An Eternal Religion

Another distinctive feature of Islam is that it not only proclaims its universal character, but also lays claims to being eternal, and it then proceeds to fulfil the preconditions of such a claim, for instance, a Message can be eternal only if it is complete and perfect in every aspect, and also guaranteed with regard to the verity of its contents. In other words, its revealed Books should bear divine guarantee against human revision and tampering. In so far as the teachings of the Holy Quran are concerned, the Almighty Himself claims in it:

اَلْيَوْمَ اَكْمَلْتُ لَكُمْ دِيْنَكُمْ وَاَتْمَمْتُ عَلَيْكُمْ نِعْمَتِیْ
وَرَضِيْتُ لَكُمُ الْاِسْلَامَ دِيْنًا

*I have this day perfected your faith for you in every way and,
having completed My bounty upon you, have chosen for you Islam
as religion.*[12]

Safeguarding of the Holy Quran

As I have already said, for a teaching to be eternal, it is not sufficient
merely that it should be complete and perfect, but that there should
also exist a guarantee for its perpetual preservation in its original form.
The Holy Quran amply satisfies this fundamental requirement, and
the One Who sent down the Holy Quran has proclaimed it in the
clearest terms that:

اِنَّا نَحْنُ نَزَّلْنَا الذِّكْرَ وَ اِنَّا لَهُ لَحٰفِظُوْنَ ۝

We have sent down this Book and verily We shall safeguard it.[13]

In other words, God Himself will safeguard it and will never allow it
to be tampered with. One method of the preservation of the text has
been that in accordance with Divine Will, there have always been
hundreds of thousands of people in every age who have committed the
text of the Holy Quran to memory, and this practice continues to this
day. And the principle measure of safeguarding the real import and
essence of the Message has been the Divine practice of appointing
guides, reformers and revivers in the latter ages. They would be
commissioned as spiritual leaders by the Almighty Himself and under
Divine guidance would settle differences and controversies among the

followers of Islam, thus safeguarding the true spirit of the Holy Quran.

Of course, there is the question as to whether the Quranic claim of its preservation is also supported by reliable corroborative evidence?

A clue to the answer to this question lies in the fact that there are a very large number of non-Muslim researchers who, despite themselves, have totally failed to show that the text of the Holy Quran has been tampered with, in the slightest manner after the passing away of the Holy Prophet[sa] of Islam. In fact, there are many non-Muslim researchers who have felt compelled, after their extensive searches in this field, to affirm openly that the Holy Quran has indeed been preserved and safeguarded in its original form. For instance, Sir William Muir in his work *The Life of Muhammad* says:

> We may, upon the strongest presumption, affirm that every verse is the genuine and unaltered composition of Muhammad himself.[14]

> Also, there is otherwise every security, internal and external, that we posses the text which Muhammad himself gave forth and used.[15]

Noldeke Says:

> Slight clerical errors there may have been, but the Holy Quran of Uthman contains none but genuine elements, though some times in very strange order. The efforts of European scholars to prove the existence of later interpolations in the Holy Quran have failed.[16]

A Complete Religion

As regards to Islam's distinctive and unique claim that the teachings of the Holy Quran are complete and perfect and fully capable of guiding humanity in all ages, this too, is fully capable of guiding humanity in all ages and is also fully supported by reason. It is not possible in a brief space of time to deal with this subject in detail, and I must confine myself to a brief reference to some guiding principles and illustrative examples. First, we must consider how Islam succeeds in meeting the demands of changing times, thus forestalling the need for any revision in its teachings. It is indeed fascinating to study Islam's practical guidance in this regard of which I shall now place a mere sample before you:

- ❖ Islam only enunciates fundamental principles and refrains from stipulating such detail as would need to vary to cope with changing times and situations.
- ❖ Islam is fully mindful of man's intellectual, social and political evolution, and its teachings cater for all possible situations. It not only recognises the fact that there occurs continuous change and development among nations, but also the reality that not all people are at par in their state of development at a given point in time . For example, it is possible that the earth may still in part be inhabited by the people of the Stone Age, and some groups and tribes may still be a thousand years behind our age, even though we share the same time. Their intellectual, social and political state may really belong to an age left far behind. I am sure we would all agree that it would be the height of folly to force modern political ideologies upon

the original inhabitants of Australia, or the pygmies of the Congo.

❖ Islam is a religion that conforms to human nature and fulfils all human needs. No change in its teachings is necessary, unless there also occurs a fundamental change in human nature, a prospect we can dismiss outright.

These were a few facets of the principles of Islamic teachings. I shall now discuss them a little further so that my submission may be understood more fully.

Zakat versus Interest

Islam condemns the institution of interest in all its forms and strongly urges its total elimination. The motive force it presents in place of interest, to move the economic wheel, is called *Zakat*.

Obviously, I cannot treat this subject in detail in the time available, and will, therefore, just say a few words on the methodology adopted by the Holy Quran to present the essence of its teachings in this important sphere.

Zakat is a system of taxing capital, realised from the well-to- do. Apart from meeting the demands of the state, this tax is intended to meet the needs of the poor. In other words, this system not only meets the requirements of the government machinery, but also guarantees to fulfil the demands of social welfare. All that has been done is to lay down the basic principle, leaving it to those with insight and understanding to settle the details in accordance with the conditions prevailing in a particular environment at a given time.

The Holy Quran says that in the wealth of those who possess over and beyond their basic needs, is also the share of those who are unable to meet their basic needs and are considered deprived in their environment. This clearly establishes that it is the right of every person to have certain basic necessities of life provided to him in every land and society, and those made responsible for meeting this obligation are the ones who possess more than their basic needs, leaving it to the state to decide upon the modus operandi, which is to ensure that the system is fair, just and equitable and adequately fulfils its basic purpose.

Directions in Political Matters

The other major international question confronting us today is that of the determination of the form of government for a given region or country. Here, too, the guiding principles of Islam are so pertinent, weighty and elastic that their truth and practicability become self-evident. No one can deny that a particular form of government so considered suitable or unsuitable only when applied to a specific set of conditions, and it is idle to imagine that a particular political system can fulfil the needs of all people for all times.

This is why Islam does not specify a particular government. It neither presents a democratic or socialist form, nor recommends kingship or dictatorship. Instead of dilating upon the methods of establishing governments, Islam enunciates the principle of conducting political and governmental affairs in a specific manner, and imposes the condition that, no matter what the form, the responsibilities of a government will always be discharged justly, and fairly, with sympathy; always fulfilling and upholding basic human rights. Thus, instead of emphasising the first segment of the commonly accepted definition of democracy, i.e., government, by the people, Islam emphasises that, whatever the form of the government, it must in all events be for the people. So when democracy is mentioned among other forms of government the real stress is laid on its quality. It is emphasised that it should not be a hollow democracy, but that those electing their rulers should be competent people, motivated in all honesty to elect only those who are really fit and equal to the task. This has been made a prerequisite of any election to office by the Holy Quran:

اِنَّ اللّٰهَ يَاۡمُرُكُمۡ اَنۡ تُؤَدُّوا الۡاَمٰنٰتِ اِلٰۤى اَهۡلِهَا ۙ وَاِذَا حَكَمۡتُمۡ
بَيۡنَ النَّاسِ اَنۡ تَحۡكُمُوۡا بِالۡعَدۡلِ ؕ ...

Verily, Allah commands you to give over the trusts to those entitled to them, and that, when you judge between men, you judge with justice. ...[17]

And then, whatever government may as a result be established, it is obliged to govern with justice, without any discrimination of race, colour, or creed.

Now I shall briefly summarise the rules that flow from the fundamentals given in the Holy Quran about any system of government:

- ❖ A government is duty-bound to protect the honour, life and property of its people.[18]
- ❖ A ruler must always act with justice, between individuals and between people.[19]

- National matters should be settled by consultation.[20]
- Government must arrange to fulfil the basic needs of man: that is to say, provide him food, clothing and shelter.[21]
- People should be provided a peaceful and secure environment, and their lives, property and honour protected.[22]
- The economic system should be equitable and orderly.[23]
- Health care should be organised.[24]
- There should prevail total religious freedom.[25]
- A vanquished people must be dealt with justly.[26]
- Prisoners of war should be treated with compassion.[27]
- Treaties and agreements must always be honoured.[28]
- Iniquitous agreements must not be forced upon the weak.[29]
- Muslim subjects are enjoined to obey the government in authority. The only exception to this rule is a case where the government blatantly opposes and prevents the carrying out of religious duties and obligations.[30]
- If differences should arise with the ruler, then these should be settled in the light of the principles enunciated in the Holy Quran and by the Holy Prophet[sa]. In no event should one be swayed by selfish motives.[31]
- People are enjoined to assist the authorities by supporting schemes that aim to promote general well-being and welfare. It is forbidden to launch so-called non-cooperation movements.[32]
- Similarly, governments are obliged to assist in beneficent undertakings, whether individual or collective, and not to obstruct such endeavours.
- A powerful country is forbidden from all forms of aggression against another country. Recourse to arms is permitted in self-defence only.[33]

Islamic Concept of Justice

I shall now cite a few important examples of Islamic principles, which perhaps need particular emphasis in the world today. The first concerns Islamic teaching in respect of equity and justice. Other religions do not present a comprehensive direction about the administration of justice and fair play, and even if they mention this at all, it is in terms that can scarcely be applicable to us today. In fact, some parts of these directions appear to conflict directly with the intellect and sensibilities of our age, and one cannot but conclude that these teachings have either become corrupted or were intended only for local and temporary application. As Judaism presents God as only the God of Israel to the exclusion of every one else, no wonder then, that it does not even in passing deal with the fundamental question of Human Rights as such.

As for Hinduism it seems outright hostile not only to the non-Hindu but also to the Hindu of a low caste, hence narrowing further the field of God's mercy to a much smaller section of the human race. Hinduism decrees:

> If a Brahmin is unable to return a loan to one of low caste, the other has no right to demand its return. But if one of low caste is unable to return a loan taken from a Brahmin, he is to be made to work as a labourer for Brahmins till such time as he is able to pay back the loan in full.[34]

Again, in Judaism we fail to detect a concept of justice toward one's enemy. It is said:

And when your Lord your God gives them over to you, and you defeat them: then you must utterly destroy them: you shall make no covenant with them.[35]

I shall now, by way of comparison, cite a few examples of Islamic teachings in the same areas. The Holy Quran enjoins, and I quote:

- ❖ And when you judge between people, do so fairly and justly.[36]
- ❖ Be strict in observing justice, and be witness for Allah, even though it be against yourselves or against your parents or kindred.[37]
- ❖ And let not a people's enmity incite you to act otherwise than with justice. Be always just, that is nearer to righteousness.[38]
- ❖ And fight in the way of Allah against those who fight against you but do not transgress. Surely, Allah loves not the transgressors.[39]
- ❖ And if they incline towards peace, incline thou also towards it.[40]

The other example I wish to cite of the eternal teachings of Islam is the one concerning revenge and forgiveness. When we compare Islam's teachings in this sphere with that of other faiths, we are at once struck by this injunction of the Old Testament:

Your eye shall not pity: it shall be life for life, eye for eye, tooth for tooth, hand for hand, foot for foot.[41]

Doubtless, such emphasis on vengeance causes not mere wonder, but also saddens our heart. However, I am not citing this example to castigate another teaching, but to show that, when viewed in the light of the Quranic principles, even such drastic measures may also sometimes be justified. The Holy Quran, thus helps us in following the conflicting teachings of other faiths in a spirit of sympathy and understanding, which, too, is an exclusive feature of Islam. According to the Holy Quran, the extraction of full vengeance was decreed only to meet the specific needs of a particular period. This was necessary to give heart to the Israelites to make them stand up for their rights after they had remained victimized and enslaved for a prolonged period, and had as a result, become cowardly and developed a deep-seated complex of being an inferior people. Obviously, in such a situation, it* would only have made the Israelites sink deeper into their morass and not give them the confidence and courage to break the shackles of abject bondage. This teaching, therefore, was right and proper in the situation, which then existed, and was indeed given by the All-Wise God.

On the other hand when we consider the New Testament, we find that in contradiction of the previous Scripture, the Old Testament, it emphasizes forgiveness to such an extent that it totally deprives the Israelites of the right to extract any vengeance whatsoever. The real reason for this was that practising the previous teaching over a long period of time, the Israelites had become hardhearted and ferocious, and this could only be remedied by suspending for a certain period their right to extract vengeance. This is why Jesus admonished them:

You have heard that it was said, 'an eye for an eye, and a tooth for a tooth', but I say to you do not resist one who is evil. But if anyone

---

* The teachings regarding forgiveness. [Publishers]

strikes you on the right cheek, turn to him the other also, and if anyone would use you and take your coat, let him have your cloak as well.[42]

Islam holds these two opposing teachings to be complementary, each suited to the conditions and situation prevailing at the time, and neither, therefore, able to lay claim to being universal or eternal. This perfectly stands to reason, for man was still progressing through earlier stages of development and had not yet become one community to which could be vouchsafed a law that would be final and universal. We believe that Islam is that final law and presents a teaching not influenced by place or time which fact is amply illustrated by its teaching in the matter being considered. The Holy Quran says:

وَجَزٰٓؤُا۟ سَيِّئَةٍ سَيِّئَةٌ مِّثْلُهَا ۖ فَمَنْ عَفَا وَاَصْلَحَ فَاَجْرُهٗ عَلَى اللّٰهِ ۗ
اِنَّهٗ لَا يُحِبُّ الظّٰلِمِيْنَ ۝

Remember that the recompense of an injury is an injury the like thereof; but whoso forgives and thereby brings about a reformation, his reward is with Allah. Surely, Allah loves not wrongdoers.[43]

Islam thus combines the best features of both the earlier teachings; with the vital addition that forgiveness is commended provided it is likely to result in an improvement and in the correction of the defaulter, that being the real objective. If not, then punishment is held to be necessary, but not exceeding the degree to which one is wronged. Surely, this guidance is in full conformity with human nature and is as practicable today as when it was revealed, fourteen centuries ago.

Some Other Distinctions

The subject of Islam's distinctive features is a very vast one, and I have been able to deal with only just a few aspects that I had chosen for this presentation. Time will permit no more than a passing reference for certain other aspects which I would not wish to omit;

* Islam holds God to be the Creator of the universe and presents His Unity in stark simple terms, comprehensible and appealing both to a rustic and an intellectual. Islam calls God a Perfect Being, the fountainhead of all Excellencies and free of all blemishes. He is a living God Who manifests Himself everywhere and Who loves His creation and listens to their supplications. He, therefore, communicates with mankind as before, and has not barred the avenues to reach Him directly.

* Islam holds that there is no contradiction between God's word and His deed. It, thus, frees us from the traditional rivalry between science and religion, and does not require man to believe in anything beyond the law of nature determined by Him. He urges us to ponder over nature and to put it too beneficent use, for everything has been created for the benefit of mankind.

* Islam does not make idle claims or compel us to believe what we do not understand. It supports its teachings with reason and explanation, satisfying our intellect and also the depths of our soul.

* Islam is not based on myths or folklore. It invites everyone to experiment for himself and holds that truth is always verifiable, in one form or another.

❖ The revealed Book of Islam is unique, distinguishing it from all other faiths. Despite their collective efforts over centuries, its opponents have not been able to equal even a small portion of this wondrous Book. Its merit lies not only in its unique literary excellence, but also in the simplicity and comprehensiveness of its teachings. The Holy Quran proclaims that it is the best teaching—a claim made by no other revealed book.

❖ The Holy Quran claims that it combines the best features of earlier scriptures, and all enduring and comprehensive teaching has been placed within its fold. The Holy Quran says:

> *Herein are lasting commandments.*[44]

> *And this indeed is what is taught in former Scriptures—*
> *The Scriptures of Abraham and Moses.*[45]

❖ A distinctive feature of Islam is that its revealed Book is in a living language. Is it not curious that the languages of all other revealed Books are either dead or no longer in general use? A living Book, it seems, had to be in a living and ever-enduring language.

❖ Another distinction of Islam is that its Prophet[sa] passed through every imaginable stage of human experience, starting from an impoverished and orphaned childhood and ending up as the undisputed ruler of his people. His life has been documented in minute detail and reflects unparalleled faith in God and constant sacrifice in his way. He lived a full and eventful life packed with action, and has left behind an example of perfect conduct in every sphere of human endeavour. This is only fitting and proper, as he was a living interpretation of the Holy Quran and by personal example lighted the way of mankind for all time to come—a role not fulfilled adequately by any other Prophet.

❖ Another distinction of Islam is its many prophecies that have been fulfilled over the ages and have reinforced the faith of its followers in the existence of the All-Knowing and Living God. This process continues to this day, as witnessed by the recent discovery of the preserved body of the Pharaoh who had driven Moses[as] and his people out of Egypt. Another fresh example of the Quranic prophecy is about the development of new means of destruction, where fire would be locked in minute particles, which would stretch and agitate before exploding with a ferocity that would cause mountains to evaporate.

❖ Another feature of Islam is that when it talks of the hereafter and life after death, it also prophesies future events of this world, the fulfilment of which reinforces the faith of its followers in life after death.

❖ Islam is distinct from other faiths in providing a comprehensive code of conduct on individual, collective and international dealings. These directions encompass every imaginable situation and include the relationship between the young and the old, the employer and the employee, among family members, between friends and partners, and even between adversaries. The rules and principles enunciated are truly universal and have already stood the test of time.

❖ Islam proclaims complete equality among mankind, irrespective of differences of caste, creed and colour. The only criterion of honour it accepts is that of righteousness, not of birth, riches, race or colour. The Holy Quran says:

$$... \; اِنَّ اَكْرَمَكُمْ عِنْدَ اللهِ اَتْقٰىكُمْ \; ...$$

...Verily, the most honourable among you, in the sight of Allah, is he who is the most righteous among you. ... [46]

And again:

$$... \; وَمَنْ عَمِلَ صَالِحًا مِّنْ ذَكَرٍ اَوْ اُنْثٰى وَهُوَ مُؤْمِنٌ فَاُولٰٓئِكَ يَدْخُلُوْنَ$$
$$الْجَنَّةَ يُرْزَقُوْنَ فِيْهَا بِغَيْرِ حِسَابٍ ٥$$

Whoso does good, whether male or female, and is believer—these will enter the Garden; they will be provided therein without measure. [47]

- ❖ Islam presents a definition of good and evil that distinguishes it from all other faiths. It does not hold natural human desires to be evil. Islam teaches that our natural inclinations should be regulated and channelled so as to make them constructive and beneficent for society.

- ❖ Islam has not only made women heirs to property, but has also given them equal rights with men and not in a manner that would disregard the distinctive features of their anatomy and their exclusive responsibilities in the bearing and nursing of children.

A Religion of Peace

In the end, I would give all seekers of peace the glad tidings that Islam alone is the faith that guarantees peace in all spheres and at all levels: individual, social, economic, national and supranational. Islam alone bears a name, the literal meaning of which is 'Peace', and one, who becomes a Muslim, not only enters a safe haven himself but also guarantees it for others, and shuns all actions that might lead to iniquity and disruption. The Holy Prophet[sa] said that a Muslim is he whose word and deed do not harm others.[48] The momentous address of the Holy Prophet[sa] delivered shortly before his death, and after the performance of what has come to be called the Farewell Pilgrimage, is an eternal Charter of Peace for all mankind. Islam enjoins peace not only between men, but also between man and his Maker, so that not only other men remain unharmed from the word and deed of a Muslim, but he himself remains safe from God's wrath and censure, the recompense which is merited as a result of committing transgression. So, a Muslim's peace is obtained in this world and also extends to the hereafter.

Islam's teachings, if followed by the nations of the world, are fully capable of saving them from strife and destruction. Islam is a living faith and claims to be able to place the relationship of man with God on the same plane as it was in the days long past. Islam does not consider revelation and communion with God to be a thing of the past. It believes that the avenues of spiritual bliss trodden upon by Noah[as], Abraham[as], Moses[as], Jesus[as] and, above all, the Prophet[sa] of Islam, are still open and beckoning to those desirous of close communion with God.

The Ahmadiyya Movement

The Ahmadiyya Movement in Islam believes that these claims have been fulfilled in our age in the person of its founder Haḍrat Mirza Ghulam Ahmad[as] who was born in 1835 in the remote village of Qadian in India. He was enabled by Divine mercy to tread the path of piety and righteousness, and, strictly following the teachings of Islam, was blessed with intimate communion with the Almighty. He received Divine revelation, which also formed the basis of his many prophecies, whose unfailing fulfilment has continued beyond his life.

In accordance with Divine direction, he founded the Ahmadiyya Movement in Islam in the year 1889, and, leaving behind a dedicated and vibrant Community of disciples numbering several hundred thousands, he departed from this earthly abode in 1908. His mission continues, and the Community has all along been headed by elected successors.

While describing his mission, the founder of our Movement had said:

> I have been sent that I should prove that Islam alone is a living religion. And I have been blessed with spiritual powers that render helpless those of other faiths, and also those from among us who are spiritually blind. I can demonstrate to every opponent that the Holy Quran is a miracle in its teachings, its enlightened knowledge, its deep and delicate insight, and in its perfect eloquence. It excels the miracles of Moses, and those of Jesus a hundred fold.[49]

He goes on to say:

I am the light in the darkness of this age. He who follows me, will be saved from the pits and ditches dug by the Devil to ensnare those straying in the dark. He has sent me so that I should lead the world, gently and in peace, to the One True God, and re-establish the moral excellences of Islam. And I have been given heavenly signs to satisfy those who seek the truth.[50]

I now end my address with another quotation from the writings of the founder of the Ahmadiyya Movement, which is a call to the whole of mankind:

The mirror which enables you to behold That Lofty Being, is His communion with man..........Let one whose heart yearns for the truth, stand up and search. I tell you in all truth, that if souls search honestly and hearts really thirst for the truth, then men should look for the right method and the right path. But how will this open, and how will this veil be lifted? I assure all seekers that Islam alone gives the glad tidings of this path, for others have long since placed a seal on God's revelation. But, be assured that God has not placed this seal: this is a mere excuse conjured up by man in his deprivation.

Verily, as it is not possible to see without our eyes, or hear without our ears, in exactly the same way, it is impossible to behold the countenance of That Beloved, without the help of the Holy Quran. I was a young man, and now I am grown old, but I have never found anyone who has drunk of the ultimate spiritual elixir, except from this holy spring.[51]

Doubtless, this call is a life-giving message for every soul that seeks the real truth.

REFERENCES

1. The Holy Quran 35:25.
2. Chronicles 16:36.
3. Samuel 25:32.
4. Matthew 15:21-25.
5. Gotama Smriti:12.
6. The Holy Quran 34:29.
7. The Holy Quran 7:159.
8. The Holy Quran 81:28.
9. The Holy Quran 2:286.
10. The Holy Quran 5:14.
11. The Holy Quran 98:6.
12. The Holy Quran 5:4.
13. The Holy Quran 15:10.
14. P. XXVIII.
15. P. XXVII.
16. Enc. Brit. 9th Edition under the word: The Holy Quran.
17. The Holy Quran 4:59.
18. Verily, Allah commands you to make over the trust to those entitled to them... The Holy Quran 4:59.
19. ...And that, when you judge between men, you judge with justice. The Holy Quran 4:59.
20. And whose affairs are decided by mutual consultation. The Holy Quran 42:39.
21. It is *provided* for thee that thou wilt not hunger therein, nor wilt thou be naked. And that thou wilt not thirst therein, nor wilt thou be exposed to the sun. The Holy Quran 20:119-120.
22. And when he is in authority, he runs about in the land to create

disorder in it and destroy the crops and the progeny of man; and Allah loves not disorder. The Holy Quran 2:206.

23. See the Holy Quran 16:91

24. The Holy Quran 6:143.
    The Holy Quran 2:169.
    See the Holy Quran 16:91

25. There should be no compulsion in religion. The Holy Quran 2:257.

26. And let not a people's enmity incite you to act otherwise than with justice. Be *always* just, that is nearer to righteousness. The Holy Quran 5:9.

27. It does not behove a Prophet that he should have captives until he engages in regular fighting in the land. The Holy Quran 8:68.
    Then afterwards either release them as a favour or by taking ransom—until the war lays down its burdens. That is the ordinance. The Holy Quran 47:5.

28. See the Holy Quran 16:92

29. See the Holy Quran 16:93

30. Obey Allah, and obey His Messenger and those who are in authority among you. The Holy Quran 4:60.

31. And if you differ in anything among yourselves, refer it to Allah and His Messenger. The Holy Quran 4:60.

32. And help one another in righteousness and piety; but help not one another in sin and transgression. The Holy Quran 5:3.

33. And strain not thy eyes after what we have bestowed on some classes of them to enjoy for a short time. The Holy Quran 20:132.

34. Manu Smriti 10:35.

35. Deuteronomy 7:2.

36. The Holy Quran 4:59.

37. The Holy Quran 4:136.

38. The Holy Quran 5:9.

39. The Holy Quran 2:191.

40. The Holy Quran 8:62.

41. Exodus 21:24.

42. Matthew 5:35-45.

43. The Holy Quran 42:41.

44. The Holy Quran 98:4.

45. The Holy Quran 87:19-20.

46. The Holy Quran 49:14.

47. The Holy Quran 40:41.

48. *Bukhārī - Kitābul Īmān.*

49. *Anjām-i-Ātham, Ruḥānī Khazā'in* Vol. 11. pp. 345, 346.

50. *Masīh Hindustān Mein, Ruḥānī Khazā'in* Vol. 15 p. 13.

51. The Philosophy of the Teachings of Islam, *Ruḥānī Khazā'in* Vol. 10 pp. 442-443.

INDEX

SOME DISTINCTIVE FEATURES *of* ISLAM was a lecture delivered by Ḥaḍrat Mirza Tahir Ahmad[rh], Khalīfatul Masīḥ IV, of blessed memory at the University of Canberra, Australia.

The speaker builds up his lecture on the thesis that the most distinctive feature of Islam is twofold. First, it is the only religion which claims to be, and is, the final, the universal and eternal religion for all times and for all peoples. Second, it is the only religion which acknowledges, and bears witness to, the veracity of every other religions and claims that the truth is not the monopoly of Islam alone—whereas every other religion claims that it alone contains the Divine truth.

Then Ḥaḍrat Mirza Tahir Ahmad[rh] answers at some length the question that if all religions are from God then why is there any difference in religions. Moreover he argues three main points: that Islamic teachings are not only universal and eternal but are also complete, comprehensive and perfect; that the Holy Quran is the final and immutable word of God free from all human interpolation; and that the Prophet of Islam, the Holy Prophet Muhammad[sa] is the Seal of the Prophets—the best of them—and the perfect model of excellence for mankind.

In the middle part of lecture he discuses seventeen features of Islam which distinguish it from other religion and ideologies including the Islamic concept of justice and Islamic teachings regarding the form and function of government.

At the end the speaker introduces the Founder[as] of Ahmadiyya Muslim Jama'at and the Jama'at itself to his audience concluding his lecture with an excerpt from the writings of the Promised Messiah[as].

ISBN 978-1-84880-895-9

CPSIA information can be obtained
at www.ICGtesting.com
Printed in the USA
BVHW051308171121
621781BV00010B/636